THREE PRAYERS

THREE PRAYERS

Our Father
O Heavenly King
The Prayer of Saint Ephrem

by

OLIVIER CLÉMENT

Translated by
MICHAEL BRECK

ST VLADIMIR'S SEMINARY PRESS
CRESTWOOD, NEW YORK 10707

Library of Congress Cataloging-in-Publication Data

Clément, Olivier.
   [Trois prières. English]
   Three prayers: Our Father, O Heavenly King, The Prayer of Saint
Ephrem / by Olivier Clément.
      p. cm.
   ISBN 0-88141-197-3 (alk. paper)
   1. Lord's prayer—Meditations. 2. O Heavenly King—Meditations.
3. Prayer of Saint Ephrem—Meditations. I. Title: 3 prayers. II. Title.

BV230 .C63 2000
242'.7—dc21

99-054452

THREE PRAYERS

Copyright © 2000 by
ST VLADIMIR'S SEMINARY PRESS
575 Scarsdale Road, Crestwood, NY 10707
1-800-204-2665

Originally published in French under the title
Trois Prières, by Desclée de Brouwer, Paris, 1993.

ISBN 0-88141-197-3

PRINTED IN THE UNITED STATES OF AMERICA

CONTENTS

Preface

The title of this little book bears explaining.

On my own, I never would have presumed to comment on these simple and fundamental texts: the Our Father, the prayer to the Holy Spirit ("O Heavenly King..."), and the penitential prayer of St Ephrem. The first is of immeasurable value for all Christians, while the other two are drawn from the heritage of the undivided Church which the Orthodox Church has preserved and now offers to all. I have neither the "technical" expertise nor the spiritual qualifications to produce such a commentary.

Quite simply, with a desire to serve—however obsolete that term may seem—I did not shy away from specific, persistent requests to do so. My reflections on the Our Father, presented at an Orthodox youth gathering, were published by the weekly journal *France-Catholique* to whom I am grateful for their permission to reprint here. The prayer to the Holy Spirit, I presented at the behest of my friend, Fr. Nicolas Ozoline, for an Orthodox television program which aired on the very day of Pentecost.

As for the prayer of St Ephrem, my commentary began on the occasion of a discussion I was given to lead at a Trappist monastery.

I had been "mulling over" these prayers for quite some time. I continued to do so until I had reworked (almost entirely for the last two) and greatly expanded them.

The Our Father is the prayer that Christ Himself taught His disciples and which the Church has handed down to us. First and foremost, as the Fathers say (I am thinking especially of the marvelous commentary by St Maximus the Confessor), it invokes the three divine Persons and their common will, then going on to the disposition which man needs in order to enter into the trinitarian realm, to make use of time eucharistically, to seek freedom through grace and an unselfish respect for others, the rejection of ultimate apostasy, and participation in Christ's victory over hell and death.

The Spirit gives us Christ who, in turn, gives us the Spirit. We receive this Spirit "for the life of the world," within the ecclesial body of the Risen One who draws every man out of nothingness. The prayer of the Holy Spirit opens us up to this breath of life, of communion and of freedom.

But nothing that endures can be acquired without an ascesis of trust and humility—as St Seraphim of Sarov used to say, the life of a Christian consists in the "acquisition of the Holy Spirit." The penitential prayer of St Ephrem, who was known in the fourth century as "the lyre of the Holy Spirit," shows us both the obstacles and the path which leads to that rare and difficult "love" which is the "synthesis of all virtue."

Of course, I have been able to provide writings that can serve only as a doorstep. It is my own prayer that they may help those who seek to enter.

Olivier Clément

I

Our Father

Our Father,
who art in heaven,
hallowed be Thy Name,
Thy kingdom come,
Thy will be done
on earth as it is in heaven,
give us this day our daily bread
and forgive us our trespasses
as we forgive those who trespass against us,
and lead us not into temptation
but deliver us from evil.

Our Father

The Our Father is the prayer which Jesus taught his disciples and which the Church, in turn, has handed down to us. It leads us into Jesus' own prayer, one that constituted His very being. And so we must understand that all of the Church's liturgical richness and its entire ascetical and spiritual heritage are none other than the symbolic structure and the means of our encounter with Christ and of our life in Christ. The Church does not set itself up as our ultimate goal, it leads us to Christ. And Christ does not lead us to Himself but, in the Holy Spirit, He leads us to the Father.

The gospels contain two versions of the Our Father: that of Luke (11:2-4) and that of Matthew (6:9-13). From the earliest years of the Church it is Matthew's longer version, already then in liturgical usage, that was kept.

The first two requests of the Our Father can be found in the Jewish *Kaddish*, the conclusion of the Synagogue service, with which Jesus must have been familiar. As the Our Father is rooted in a very particular history—that of the Old Testament—it discloses it, surpasses and fulfills it.

The first word of the prayer taught to us by Jesus and which, in a way, we say with Him, in Him, in His Spirit, is indeed Father: *Pater hêmon* ("Our Father.") Let us pause for a moment at this word which is truly the first: "Father." It has a strange sound in our day. Contemporary man is an orphan. He has no roots outside of time and space. He feels lost in an infinite universe. Having descended from primates he moves toward nothingness.

He has been told that fatherhood within the family, or in a figurative sense in society, is absurd and "repressive." Without a doubt, it is so if it fails to convey a spiritual meaning of life: so many fathers are no more than "begetters."

He has been told that "God the Father" is the enemy of his freedom, a type of celestial spy, a sadistic, castrating father. One must admit that historically, Christendom, in the East as in the West, at one time or another has amply justified this accusation.

Thus, many now turn toward Eastern religions, to a kind of interior science that ultimately evokes an impersonal divinity resembling a sort of cosmic matrix. Yes, we are *orphans*. Incest and homosexuality, two signs of paternal absence, haunt our society. The death of the father figure takes shape in our fear of other people.

This is why today, strangely enough, there is a growing nostalgia with regard to this father figure, and why the Church teaches us this prayer that begins with the word "Father."

This Father transcends sexual duality. St John speaks of the "bosom of the Father," while the entire Bible evokes the "bosom of mercy," *rahamim*, in the sense of a womb: this Father is motherly. He "senses" his children as a mother "senses" her own, with her whole being, with all her flesh and within her bosom.

Nevertheless, He is called "Father." As this metaphor suggests, the ultimate end is not assimilation but communion, a liberating communion that enables us to make our way toward others.

Thus: "Father." How is this significant in our daily lives? It means that we are never, ever, lost orphans at the mercy of the forces and circumstances of this world. We have a *recourse*, we have an *origin* beyond time and space. This seemingly infinite universe (though according to Einstein time began with the "big bang" and space is curved and contained) has its place within the word, the breath and the love of the Father.

Nebulae and atoms (which are also nebulae) have an impersonal love for the Father, through their very existence, but we human beings are able to love Him personally. We can consciously respond to Him and express His cosmic word in such a way that each of us, by virtue of our bond with the Father, is nobler and greater than the entire world.

Faces become inscribed beyond the stars, within the love of the Father. Each one of those seemingly fleeting moments in which, as the poet would say, "our veins were flowing with being" is forever inscribed in the loving memory of the Father.

And thus the nihilism of this age is vanquished. The anguish within us can be changed to trust, and the hatred to union. What we must sense most strongly, each day—and I say this especially to those who are young—is that it is good to live. To live is grace. To live is glory. All life is a blessing.

It seems to me that in the literature of peoples influenced by Orthodoxy, even among writers who are not

firm believers (such as the earlier Tolstoy or the great Siberian novelists of old), we discover this sense for the
goodness and the deep beauty of beings and of things,
with grace at the root of it all; an infinitely merciful fatherhood giving life to all things. It is from this understanding that these writers draw their marvelous ability
to depict children and the affection between parents and
children—a rare element in contemporary Western
literature.

Our theology and our spirituality know all too well
that this mystery of our origin cannot be captured in
words or concepts. But Jesus reveals to us that this
abyss—known as such also in India—is an abyss of love
and a fatherly abyss. With Jesus—in Him, in His
breath—we dare to stammer: "*Abba,* Father." It is a word
of infinite, child-like tenderness, of a trust imbued with
respect: this is the whole Christian paradox. Nevertheless, Jesus reveals to us that this paradoxical relationship
exists not only in the relationship of the Father with creation but also within God Himself, as a fundamental trait
of the absolute. Within God is the unoriginate cause, the
filial Other and the Breath of life and of love that rests on
the Other and leads Him, and us in Him, back to the origin of all. Within God is the breath of love, the great mystery of unity and diversity, and we, made in the image of
God, are swept up in this rhythm.

But with God the response of love, between the Cause
and His filial Other, in their unifying Breath, is immedi-
ate. The reciprocity of their love is absolute. Whereas for
us there is a need for time, for space and for a kind of
darkness in order for us to move both toward the Light

and toward one another. We are often like the prodigal son who squanders his fortune with prostitutes and tends to the pigs, envious of their fare. But even then we know not only that the Father awaits us but that He is coming out to meet us. The world is not a prison but a dark passage—an opening through which to move, a passage to be deciphered within a greater work. In this work, everything has a meaning, everyone is important, everyone is necessary. It is a work that we compose together with God.

Because the Father blesses all things, we must, in turn, learn to bless Him in all things. We must first attempt to recover, renew and inwardly relive all the formulaic blessings taught to us by the Church and that connect us to the divine blessings of the first chapters of Genesis: "and God saw that it was good." The Septuagint translates *tob*, which means "good and beautiful," as *kalon*, "beautiful." Maximus the Confessor teaches us to find in every attentive and contemplative observation of things a kind of trinitarian experience. The very fact that a thing exists leads us back to the Father, the "creator of heaven and earth and of all things visible and invisible..." (thus, everything becomes the *visible of the invisible*). The fact that we are able to understand this thing, to discern within it and perceive from it a phenomenally "intelligent" structure, leads us back to the Son, the Word, Wisdom and Reason of the Father. The fact that it is a thing of beauty, that it is dynamically integrated into a given order and tends toward fullness, leads us back to the Spirit, to the life-giving Breath which Sergius Bulgakov described as the personification of beauty. Let us learn to discern the Fatherhood of God in all things, the Father and "His two hands," the Word and the Spirit, as St Irenaeus of Lyons says, the Father together with His Wisdom and His Beauty.

Nevertheless, the most fundamental trinitarian experience is inscribed in the *hémon* that follows the *Pater,* the second word of the Our Father: "Father *of us*."

Concerning this "us," I would like to make two points.

The first is that we must learn to discern *the mystery of God in the face of our neighbor*. The horror of history, particularly in this century, is that man has at times laid claim to absolute power over others. Various ideologies claim to explain man, reducing him to race, class, ethnicity, religion or culture. Those who produce these ideologies, "those who know," thus feel justified, for the good of humanity, as they say, in manipulating, conditioning, imprisoning, torturing and killing others. This may be the result of a modern frame of mind that seeks to grasp everything (this is precisely the usage of the German word *Begriff,* which means "concept").

Over against this notion we must understand that, whoever they may be—publicans, prostitutes or Samaritans, as Jesus says (we can easily interpret His meaning)—all people are the image of God, children of the Father. They are as unexplainable and "inconceivable" as God Himself, and there is no better description than that they are indefinable. Let us learn to stop detesting and scorning others. As one desert Father has said: "there is no other virtue than to refrain from scorning others." The other is a countenance, his whole being is a countenance; and before a countenance I have no power. Because this countenance is also a word, I can only attempt to respond and become responsible. This is true for relationships of love, of friendship and of collaboration; within families as well as in society; in our relationships with other Christians as well as in the realm of politics. Remember: refrain from scorning others!

The other point I'd like to emphasize and which, furthermore, is inseparable from the first, is the relationship between the Church and mankind: "Father *of us*." Is this "*us*" just the Church where we are all "members of one another": a single body, one being in Christ, with each of us encountering Jesus personally, each of us being illumined by the one pentecostal flame? The Word, as the Prologue of John says, "is the true light that enlightens every man who comes into the world." This has also been translated as: "...that, coming into the world, enlightens every man." In becoming incarnate, the Word assumed all of humanity, every person from every time and place. In His resurrection He raised all mankind.

Whether they are many or few, the Church is comprised of those who discover all this, who lucidly enter into this light and give thanks on behalf of all. The Church is the "royal priesthood," the "holy nation" set apart to pray, to bear witness and to work for the salvation of all mankind. We know where the heart of the Church is: it is in the Gospel and in the Eucharist. And yet we remain unaware of the extent to which it enlightens because the Eucharist is offered "for the life of the world."

There is not one blade of grass that does not grow within the Church and not one constellation that does not revolve within it around the tree of the Cross, the new tree of life and the world's axis. There is not one person who does not have a mysterious relationship with the Father who created him, with the Son, the "ultimate man," and with the Breath that moves all living things. There is not one person who does not aspire to goodness, who does not tremble before beauty, nor is there one who is devoid of a sense of mystery when faced with love and with death.

On the day of judgment, as they are filled with joy, many will say: "Lord, when did we see you hungry and give you food...a stranger and welcome you, naked and clothe you? When did we see you in prison or sick and visit you?" And they will hear it said to them: "Truly, I say to you, as you did it to the least of these little ones, my brothers, you did it to me!" Are we doing these things?

Let us not, in our daily lives, turn the Church into a sect or a ghetto. Let us learn to discern the seeds of life in all things. Let us learn to welcome them into our understanding and our love and to gather them into our prayer within the Church.

Our Father who art in heaven

"Heaven" refers here to the inaccessible and abyss-like character of the Father, a God beyond God; *hypertheos*, according to the Areopagite. We draw near to Him by probing his absence. This is the negative theology to which I referred earlier: the mind assesses its own limitations, always perceiving afar off, the murmur of the divine ocean.

Then comes the moment when all mental activity ceases, when man withdraws himself, falls silent and becomes pure expectation. We need these moments of silent awareness in our daily lives. The Fathers speak, for example, of the awareness that takes hold of us when, from the edge of a cliff, we see the whirling sea stretch out in front of us.

We must learn at times to stop and listen to the silence, to savor it and be awed by it, becoming like a chalice to receive it. This might happen during a calm moment at home or alone in a room, in a church that stands open in a city or during a walk in the woods. It might be in the Gospel which we must try to read every day, in a psalm, in a text or in a word that touches our heart and transfixes us: then we go no further, we pause in silent, at times overwhelming anticipation...

But why precisely is the *sky* used as a symbol for transcendence? No doubt because its deep hue (especially in Mediterranean countries) is both ubiquitous and beyond our reach, encompassing and penetrating all things with its light. In archaic languages, the word used to designate the divinity means "brilliant sky."

We must learn to observe the sky, allowing ourselves to be overtaken and cleansed by it to the depths of our souls so to speak. Why do so many young people, who never go to church, climb mountains and high places if not, in some way, to reach the sky? Why do they venture toward the southern seas where water and sky are melded into a "complete" sphere?

"We have found it. What? Eternity. It is the sea mingled with the sun."

And yet, the overwhelming revolution of the modern age has been the discovery of an empty and infinite space where neither God nor man seem to have a proper place.

The rejoicing heavens depicted in the Psalms and the book of Job have become a dark void. In vain, Nietzsche, in his madness, seeks God in a world that is pathetically adrift, a world that has lost all sense of direction and is growing colder and colder. Thus, the emotion brought about by a brilliant blue sky may come to be no more than part of one's holiday entertainment. The divine heaven must be found elsewhere.

Elsewhere? The ascetics say in the "heart," in the innermost center, in the greatest depth where our whole being comes together and opens onto an abyss of light: the *inner heaven*, the color of sapphire, according to Evagrius of Pontus.

One of our daily tasks is precisely to awaken in our selves the power within the depths of our heart. Usually, we live in our heads and in our sexuality, with our hearts closed off. But only the heart can serve as the crucible in which our understanding and desire are transformed. And though we may not reach the luminous abyss, sparks may fly from it, and our hearts burn with an immense yet gentle shudder.

We must recover the meaning of this unemotional emotion, this unsentimental sentiment, this peaceful and overwhelming resonance of our whole being we feel when our eyes are filled with tears of wonder and gratitude, ontological tenderness and fulfilled silence. It is not merely the concern of monks; it is humbly and partially the concern of us all. And I would add that it is also a question of *culture*.

In Solzhenitsyn's *Cancer Ward*, a young woman in charge of part of the hospital asks her superior, the "old doctor," whence comes his ability for sympathy and, therewith, his assurance in giving a diagnosis. He answers that for some time he was deepened and enlightened by the love of a woman and that, if it is the rare grace of knowing that another person exists, love can indeed penetrate a "heart of stone" and change it into a "heart of flesh."

But, the "old doctor" adds, it has been years since this woman died. Now, at times, he has to withdraw, lock himself in and find inner silence, allowing his heart to find peace and become like the smooth surface of a lake reflecting the moon and the stars. This silence and peace enable the Father "who is in heaven" to draw near. And on the mirror of the heart that receives him is inscribed the truth of all things.

There is also a question of culture. We need music, poems, novels, songs and any art that has the potential to be popular art and which awakens the power within our hearts.

At times, in the metro in Paris, a song from the high plains of South America catches my attention as it follows the meandering boundary between death and love, between revolt and celebration.

There is also the great love-story of Arabic literature: that of Majnûn and Laylâ. Majnûn, the madman, loves Laylâ—night. Laylâ loves Majnûn but, without revealing her secret, in the shape of a gazelle, she disappears into the desert. Henceforth Majnûn is destined to wander...and sing. We need Majnûn's song. We need a kind of beauty that is not possessive, as is so often the case in our day, but precisely one of *dis*-possession and perhaps of communion, "the beauty which creates communion," as the Areopagite says.

St John Climacus refers to "those *profane* melodies that bear us up to inner joy, divine love and blessed tears." The secret genius of Christianity is "philokalian." "Philokalia" means "love of beauty." This beauty must not be limited to the liturgy or to ascesis but should also radiate throughout our culture.

Hallowed be Thy Name

From all eternity the Father makes His name known in his Word. The Word is made flesh in order that this Name might be revealed to us and wholly blessed, for the Name is at once a "separate" and a radiant presence, that is *holy*. In Christ's time, "blessing the Name" did not refer to the honor and praise given to God but to the giving of one's life, to martyrdom. Jesus blessed the Name all the way to the cross, and the Name blessed Him unto the resurrection. As the Byzantine liturgy states: when Jesus is crucified, it is "One of the Holy Trinity" that is crucified. When Jesus is crucified, God is crucified.

In this complete subjection to the cross the Name of God is revealed. And this Name is love, "God is love," as St John says. In His love for us, God joins us in our suffering, in our rebellion, in our despair and our agony: "My father, if it be possible, let this cup pass from me." "My God, my God, why have you forsaken me?" Thus, henceforth, the incarnate and crucified God comes between our suffering and the void, between our rebellion, our despair, our agony and the void and, rising from the dead, opens for us strange passages of light.

For us to "bless the Name," we have only to *take refuge in the cross of Christ*. Christian martyrdom is a mystical experience in which a person, at the moment of greatest suffering, gives himself over to a humble trust in Christ. It is then that he becomes suffused with the joy of the resurrection.

They are many ways to be a martyr: "blessed are those who are persecuted for righteousness sake... blessed are you when men shall persecute you..." Or, quite simply, in sickness, in waning, in losing our loved ones, in betrayal, loneliness and death.

First of all, for one's neighbor as well as for oneself, one must give especially attentive care to the struggle against suffering.

The modern West has done much in this area, to its credit, for suffering can be dark, senseless and infernal: it becomes so often a separation, an obsession, a death prior to death. If it is more moderate, and if we live in faith, it can turn our bodies into monastic cells in which we become detached and open.

Yet, above all, I must pray that I may live my ultimate suffering and die my death, mysteriously identifying my body with Christ's tortured body, so that there may arise in me the "blessing of the Name," and even, God willing, that it shine forth from me as if (to borrow St Paul's expression) I were in a way completing that which was lacking in the suffering of Christ. Then, perhaps, through the anguish and the horror, a light may filter down and with Jesus, in Him, I may be able to say not only "my God, my God, why have you forsaken me?", but also "Father, into your hands I commend my spirit."

I say all this in the first person. For others, I don't know, there are only specific instances. Christianity does not entail omniscience. It may mean knowing nothing, yet trusting nonetheless.

About "blessing the Name" I would like to make two further points:

The first is that the Name both *invokes and evokes the Presence*. It does not have a grasp of this presence, as with magic, but offers us up to it. Those who begin to love one another exchange names, while the one often thinks of the name of the other. The same is true of our relationship with Christ, though it is infinitely stronger, for at least with Him we are certain of His love.

We know more or less what is referred to as the "Jesus Prayer," ("Lord Jesus Christ, Son of God, have mercy upon me, a sinner."), uttered in the rhythm of one's breathing. In ancient monasticism, we find all kinds of short formulae: "*Kyrie eleison*," "I pray Thee, O Lord, I pray Thee," "O Lord, help me, hasten to rescue me," "As you know and as you will..." "Glory to Thee, O Lord, glory to Thee," etc.

We can make up others. In our daily lives it is a simple way of "blessing the Name," of sanctifying all things with it, of marking all things with it as with an eternal seal or, through it, of discerning a given situation. Because God speaks to us continually through others, through things and through encounters... Thus the Name is shown to be inexhaustible; it is a diamond with a thousand facets, each corresponding to something, to a face, to a situation...

Certainly for most of us it not a question of perpetually maintaining the invocation of the Name, but of raising from time to time a call for help or a celebration. The point is not to forget God, for according to the spiritual masters, forgetting is the greatest sin; forgetfulness, sleepwalking, insensitivity of the soul, hardness of heart. Then, suddenly, we remember God, be it only to confront Him, as did Jacob, or to inveigh against Him, as did Job. To cry out to Him, to the Living God, and not to remain silent before the brass wall of fate, of the void and of inevitable disaster. Lord, why? "Why hast thou made me thy mark?" says Job. "How long wilt thou not...let me alone till I swallow my spittle?" Lord, come to help me. Guide me and enlighten me. Not as I will but as you will. And in joy or simply in the humble pleasure of being: Glory to Thee, O God, glory to Thee! Then we realize we had far more time to pray than we thought. The invocation of the Name is a prayer for those who have no time to pray.

The other point I would like to make concerning the "blessing of the Name" is that, for Christ, there is no static division between the sacred and the profane, and there are no rules separating what is pure from what is impure. Our daily lives evolve between the *Kiddush haschem,* "blessing the Name, and the *Hillul haschem,* "profaning the Name." The dividing line is in continual motion, passing through our hearts, through our mouths that speak what is in our hearts and through our gaze.

All things can be sanctified. As Zachariah says, "every pot...shall be sacred to the Lord of Hosts," and according to Revelation, "the honor and the glory" of the nations shall enter into the new Jerusalem. *No one is deinitively "good" or "evil"*: for a teacher, for a judge, for anyone in authority, this is the key to relationships with others.

If technology is to free us more and more from crushing physical labor or from menial tasks, it would have to be—together with an indispensable cultural revolution—so that we might recover the ability to bless the Name in conjunction with material things, in the practice of an art-form or in the serene mastery of intelligence incorporated into machines.

Thy kingdom come

After the Father and the Son, in whom He reveals His Name, comes the Holy Spirit. An ancient variant reading of Luke's Gospel replaces "Thy kingdom come" with "Thy Spirit come." *May your Holy Spirit come and bring us your Kingdom*: your glory, your energies, your grace, your light, your life, your power and your joy...all these have the same meaning. The kingdom, the new heaven and the new earth, is both heaven and earth renewed in Christ, suffused with the grace of the Spirit who is pure life; life set free from death. The world that is "in Christ" is the real "burning bush," says Maximus the Confessor. But this fire is covered with dross and ashes, the remains of our separation, of our darkness, our hatred and of all our collusion with the powers of chaos and darkness.

"Thy kingdom come" implies preparation in and anticipation of Christ's return, by removing the dross and ashes, for the kingdom whose coming we are requesting is already secretly present; every eucharistic celebration is an intimation of the *parousia*. There are eucharistic moments in the life of every person, hints of the *parousia*.

We must not fear these moments, this fullness—the *plerophoria* referred to by the spiritual masters. They are moments of silent prayer, of prayer beyond prayer, when our hearts burn within us. They are moments of creative tension or of peaceful trust, when the light of the Eighth Day shines forth in an intuition of truth and of beauty or in a genuine encounter. May we discover "the inner realm of a gaze" and "see others as a miracle"—Patriarch Athenagoras would say—or again, may we unite as we do in February for the doxology of the first almond tree to bloom. It may also be after the throes of agony have subsided and peace has come over the face of a dead person, and when (as Franz Rosenzweig says), "as a person gives up the last vestiges of individuality and returns to his origins, the Self is awakened to ultimate individuation and to ultimate solitude…"

In all these moments—and we can think of many others—the Kingdom comes mysteriously to the fore. Then a levity comes to all things; there is no more death (insofar as this term conveys the burden of the void), only *paschas*, passages. There is no more divisive exterior; the love is so great that even desire falls away, leaving only a countenance, and this whole countenance is a gaze, according to a Macarian homily. The earth is sacred, a sacrament, and the stars at night are fiery signs set out for us by the angelic realms…

Do not misunderstand me! There is also a grotesquely—rather tragically—covetous and narcissistic attitude toward pleasure, toward the delight of *being*. It is made up of the two generative passions: carnal gluttony and spiritual pride… As Kierkegaard used to say, man

runs the risk of becoming fragmented into "little eterni-
ties of delight." In things and in beings he sees only—the
language is significant here—"what is accessible to his
senses" and "what he can sink his teeth into."

But if it is experienced with a certain inner distance,
with gratitude and with respect for beings and for things
while "blessing the Name," pleasure, the delight of being,
can become a passionless joy, in the ascetical sense of the
word "passion," that is non-idolatrous. Then it is a reminder of Paradise, and an anticipation of the Kingdom. A
dance-step, the rhythm of one's breath—"to breathe, O invisible poem!" says Rilke—the smell of the earth after a
storm, a cosmic incense, the perpetual, hesychastic furling
and unfurling of the waves and the nebulae, the "Song of
Songs" from a great and noble love, where bodies are the
intimations of souls; all these can become reminders of
Paradise and anticipations of the Kingdom.

The creative act that summons beauty suffuses life
and love, the smile of an infant who discovers his own
existence through his mother's smell, through her gaze
and her voice. All this can become a reminder of Paradise, an anticipation of the Kingdom.

In the Spirit, in the great breath of the living God,
Christ's commandments—which are epitomized in the
love of God, the love of one's neighbor and of oneself (it
is so difficult to accept oneself; and yet, "you shall love
your neighbor *as yourself*")—are revealed as paths of responsibility and of communion.

The revelation of the Kingdom is indeed that there is
nothing greater than persons and communion among persons. Justice, truth and beauty are no longer laws but vital

energies; better still is our participation, through Christ's humanity, in the corresponding divine energies.

And if you do not succeed in "keeping the commandments," never consider yourself lost. Do not torment yourself in a moralizing or willful manner. Deeper still, beyond your shame and your disgrace, there is Christ. Turn to Him, let Him love you and bestow His strength upon you. There is no point in hammering away at the surface, *the heart is what must change*.

Your first task is not to try to love God but only to *understand that He loves you*. If love responds to love and you are awakened in the depth of your heart, then the very life of Christ, that is the breath of the Spirit, will arise within you. Now you have only to remove the obstacles, deviations, all the stones and silt deep within you that stop up the well-spring—though henceforth that will be your desire.

Once and for all, you will have to take a breath deeper than the air of this world, "breathe in the Holy Spirit," as Gregory of Sinai says. And may this breath within you unite with, liberate and express the lament of creation, the hope of the cosmos, which the whole Bible tells us is unfolding, in its genesis: a cosmogenesis and, ever since the Incarnation, a christogenesis (why not appropriate, outside of their dubious systematization, these beautiful terms coined buy Teilhard?); a christogenesis in which man must act like a king, a priest and a prophet...

Thy will be done on earth as it is in heaven

The will of God is not a judicial imperative, it is an influx of life; it bestows existence and renews it when it goes astray. The will of God is, first of all, creation itself, the universe itself entirely borne up by the *will-ideas*, by the *logoi*, the sustaining words of the poet-God. Then comes the history of *salvation*, the dramatic dialogue of love between God and mankind "for the salvation of all mankind," as is emphasized by the First Epistle to Timothy. This is why we must pray each day that in fact everyone be saved; we must pray for "all those who do not know how, do not want to or cannot pray for themselves."

The will of God is not done. According to Genesis, this good and beautiful world is plunged into horror. As we read in the Prologue of John, there is light, but there is also darkness. God's omnipotence is in love. And since love cannot be imposed without thereby denying it, this omnipotence—capable of creating beings that can reject it!—is also ultimate weakness. It can act only through human hearts that freely allow its light to shine through them. God respects human freedom as he respected that of the angels. But in order to keep that freedom from succumbing to the darkness, He becomes incarnate and descends into death, into hell, so that there could be a place where the will of man might unite itself to the divine will. That place is Christ. In Christ, the human will became painfully and joyously united to that of the Father. In the Risen One, seated at the right hand of the Father, the will of God is done on earth as it is in heaven.

Here again, we need only to cleave to Christ with our whole being. "Come to me, all who labor and are heavy laden, and I will give you rest. Take my yoke upon you, and learn from me; for I am gentle and lowly in heart, and you will find rest for your souls. For my yoke is easy and

my burden is light" (Mt 11:28-30). The Kingdom—
where the will of God is done on earth as it is in
heaven—"is not of this world," and it will not be realized
in history. And so the prayer to do the will of God pro-
vides us with an ironic, realistic and patient sense for politics. It "laicizes" the wielding of power and relativizes
the ideologies and raptures of history—the history of collective powers, in the Marxist sense. In our initial approach, we do not think of transforming society into
paradise but fight so that it might not become hell; we
maintain the equilibrium it needs, whether through the
"distribution of power" (*à la* Montesquieu) or the An-
glo-Saxon—and protestant—notion of "checks and bal-
ances" in the State. A man of prayer and hope avoids as
well as he can both the cynicism of conservatives (the
good management of ills considered to be inevitable, *for
others!*) and the bitterness of revolutionaries (inevitably
disappointed in both unrealized revolutions and in those
too well carried out). He knows there will be no end of
foolishness and hatred, but that is no reason to give up.
At the same time we must affirm, together with Serge
Bulgakov, that "history is not an empty corridor." This
immense power of life, of genuine life, which the Resurrection has brought to the world, which runs over from
the eucharistic chalice and the prayers of the saints, cannot be expressed merely in individual destinies. Society
and culture make up facets of a person and of interper-
sonal relationships.

Christianity has attempted, not unsuccessfully, to
sanctify culture. But more and more it has stifled freedom. Today it behooves the Church to break away from

nostalgia and from the desire for power in order to become—or become once again—the secret soil from
which the forests of the future will rise up. And she will
not be alone in this but working together with every con-
verging—primarily Christian—form of research, and
with every expectation and intuition of modern culture,
be it a renewed reflection on human rights, a *metanoia,*
sketched out in a philosophy for which anything that is
not mere trappings for the void has to do with relationships and countenance; be it the achievements of science
or even the critical study of economics.

With ideologies crumbling and nihilism on the rise,
the time is coming for a creative Christianity. Some
non-Christian thinkers, such as Gramsci and Foucault,
have suggested that the real infrastructure of history is
culture. And yet we know that culture, provided it does
not become perverted, feeds on spirituality. It is like the
tectonic plates: the deepest layers of the earth's crust
need only budge a few millimeters to cause earthquakes
on the surface. As Berdyaev would say, true revolutions
are spiritual revolutions.

In our day, Bishop Irenaeus of Crete calls it a "revolution of conscience." Religious thinkers of the first half of
this century, especially in France and in Russia, have
opened up new paths and brought about inspiration.

In the coming years there will be a need for Christian
initiatives and proposals aimed directly at culture and society at large. There will have to be Christians—working
in groups if possible, or supported by church communities—suggesting new approaches, coming up with new
ways of living and working in their jobs, in schools, in

the courts, in hospitals and in the ghettos where despair breeds violence…

There will never be a "civilization of love" in any form other than an idea or a seed. Our collective life will always be carried out against a backdrop of irrational impulses which we must learn to manage, to utilize and to contain (and here clear-headed, moderate machiavellians are better off than naive sentimentalists).

Evil can be cured at its very root only by holiness. But holiness—the Gospel—must introduce into society a certain tension, a seed, or even a wound, that makes up the very context of spiritual freedom. And even if there can never be a complete and definitive "civilization of communion," we must nonetheless persist tirelessly in opening small avenues of communication.

Give us this day our daily bread

It is from God that we ask for our bread, the bread that is for us, the bread which we need. We must do what is necessary to secure it, to obtain it honestly, through our work, in a society that hopefully is honest as well (this is a point to which I shall return). Nonetheless, we ask it of God, as a gift and as a grace. Bread is what makes me live. And yet, the fact that I am still alive today presupposes the accumulation, over several decades, of an incredible convergence of favorable circumstances! There are so many times I could have…should have died: war, accidents, heart trouble, cancer, temptation to suicide—who knows? A given person whose face, whose voice and whose prayer on my behalf are also my daily bread, could die at any moment. Or another, a child perhaps, whose future I would like to protect and guide, escapes me entirely.

There are only two possible outcomes: either anguish, with every attempt at avoiding it having little success, as we know; or prayer: our bread. The bread that is provided for us by an entire civilization, food, clothing, housing, security; the bread that we acquire through our fragile biological or psychological existence; the bread that is made up also of the many affections and impressions on which our souls feed—we recognize that it comes to us from You: give it to us this day. Or simply: *give us this day*. If it is your will, I will die today; I am a useless servant, free from this strange game that is essentially foreign to me... "Then Job arose, and rent his robe, and shaved his head, and fell on the ground and worshipped. And he said, 'Naked I came from my mother's womb, and naked I shall return; the Lord gave, and the Lord has taken away; blessed be the name of the Lord'" (Job 1:20-21).

And so we receive each day as a day of grace. But there is more. Today we ask for this bread, this sustenance, as if it were the "bread to come," the bread of the Kingdom. And yet the bread of the Kingdom is the Eucharist. What we are asking from God is that we might receive, on this day, every kind of bread, every form of sustenance, as if it were the Eucharist; that is, communion in his Body and in his Presence. In Jewish mysticism it is said that, because of our blindness, the presence, the *schekhinah*, is in exile in the secret realms of beings and of things.

The daily task of believers is to discern and set free these sparks of the Presence, that they might again return to the original fire, not by abandoning matter but by transfiguring it. In Virgil Gheorgiu's work, *The Twenty-fifth Hour*, we find a Romanian peasant eating solemnly, attentively and with gratitude, as if he were receiving communion. When a meal becomes the celebration of an encounter, its eucharistic character is augmented. St Paul says, "give thanks (*eucharisteite*) in all circumstances" (1 Thess 5:18).

There is a particular way of washing, a way of dressing, of being nourished—whether through food or through beauty—a way of welcoming one's neighbor that is eucharistic. It seems to me there is also a eucharistic way of fulfilling our dull, tiresome and repetitive daily tasks (after all the text of the *Our Father* makes reference to bread rather than wine, and bread carries with it a certain sense of necessity). We need a certain detachment and, quite simply, not to forget God, even if we have nothing to offer him but our weariness, our exhaustion or, if nothing else, our inability to offer anything.

Enable us to discern in beings, in things and in everyday situations the face and the word of the coming Christ.

According to Orthodox tradition, it is good to invoke the Holy Spirit before any task, regardless of its importance, and thereafter to sing praises to the Mother of God. She is the mother we no longer have, or never had; she is the consolation we have always sought from a woman—in vain, naturally, as a woman is also in need of consolation. She is already wholly in the Kingdom and is our help in reaching the other side. She is the ultimate synthesis, within a created person, of every tenderness and of all beauty.

The request for bread brings to mind what our relationship with the earth ought to be, because bread is the earth which we have worked. We will either destroy the earth or make her into a eucharistic offering.

The earth is no goddess. Technology has finally eradicated the "person" from the womb of mother earth. But neither is it a set of forces to be blindly exploited at the risk of compromising nature, as we see happening in our day. When it comes to the relationship of mankind with the earth, Christians must recommend, rather than economic or ecological solutions (both of which are blind), a loving and progressively transfiguring responsibility. "Our sister, mother earth," as St Francis of Assisi so beautifully put it. Our sister, our betrothed, whom we must wed with an infinite respect, so that she might produce not only our daily bread but a sweet-smelling bread bearing the full aroma of the Kingdom...

If we want to make a conscious and honest request for this bread, we must assume another obligation: that of *sharing*. Eucharistic communion is sharing. As St John Chrysostom would say, the sacrament of "one's neighbor" cannot be separated from that of "the altar." Socialist atheism and oppressive communism came about because Christians were unable to share; because they retained the sacrament of "the altar" and forgot that of "the neighbor." The tragedy, as we now can see, continues to worsen on a worldwide level.

We must first put sharing into practice from one person to another, from one family to another, and perhaps within our parishes, which we hope to see grow more or less into genuine communities. We must lay the foundation within our own environment; we must emphasize it in our social stance, at a national level, in the respect we show in welcoming foreigners and immigrants, both to assimilate and, if they so desire, to preserve their culture. Again, we must do so on the scale of the entire human race. We may dream, suggest and define an economic world order. We need stringent and realistic economists, but also ones capable of submitting their knowledge to prayer: give us—every one of us—the bread we need, and may it also be the bread of the Kingdom, the bread of fraternal benevolence and of beauty.

But since we are speaking of everyday life, we must patiently perpetuate minute accomplishments, both in rich and in poor societies, thus bringing them into dialogue with one another. Most importantly we must strive for a new way of life for which we might serve as examples. It is a way of life founded on willing moderation for the sake of sharing worldwide.

And forgive us our trespasses as we forgive those who trespass against us

"Forgive us our trespasses." We owe everything to God. We exist only through His creative will, through and for His Incarnation which opens for us the way of our fulfillment, reconciling us to Him and giving us His grace. As Philaret of Moscow has said: "all creatures rest upon the creative word of God as on a bridge of diamonds, beneath the abyss of infinite divinity, and above the abyss of their own nothingness."

Closing ourselves off and rejecting this relationship that gives us our existence amounts to giving ourselves

up to destruction and death. Strictly speaking, it is nihilism, especially if we accept Pierre Boutang's etymologi-
cal interpretation of the Latin word *nihil*: *ne-hile*, a
broken hilum, the small yet life-sustaining connection
between the grain and the stem. But even here, perhaps
especially here, in this *nihil*, the incarnate and crucified
God has descended into hell and awaits us in order to forgive us our trespasses.

We should mention Nicholas Cabasilas' striking texts
on salvation through love. He writes about Christ that He
comes to us willingly "and declares his love for us, and
prays that our love might echo His own. When He is rejected,
He does not go away, He does not take offense. When He is
pushed away, He waits at the door. Like a true lover He bears
every insult and dies"—in order to rise up and to raise us in
hopes that we might accept Him. "For all the good He has
done for us, God asks only for our love in return; in exchange
for our love, He remits our entire debt."

Cabasilas, who was himself a layman, recommends
brief meditations to those living in his day, reminders in a
way: to remember, within the time it takes to put one foot
in front of the other, that God exists and that He loves us.
I exist only through you; I exist only in you; forgive me
as I so often forget this; help me to accept myself as your
creation, as the first among sinners—a sinner who is for-
given—as a darkened and woeful member of your body,
of your Church. Help me to accept myself within the limits that you will, with the assurance that you, and you
alone, transcend all limits...

"Lord, all things are in you, even I am in you; accept
me," a character of Dostoievsky's once said. I can put

one foot in front of the other, not just in the street but in life as well, only by recalling the forgiveness and the mercy of God and His will that I live. Otherwise, through self-hatred and the perception of my own existence, I would disintegrate into nothingness; or rather, into hell.

"Forgive us our trespasses": this remembrance alone can free us from narcissism as well as from depression, the sort of weariness of our whole being, that in our day are undoubtedly the most common forms of sin.

But there is one fundamental condition to our living unfettered, in the presence of our God, and that is that we also forgive those who are in our debt.

We cannot continue without mentioning the parable of the destitute servant (Mt 18:23-35)—and we are all destitute servants! A man owed the king a tremendous sum of money which he was unable to repay. So, he was to be sold into slavery together with his entire family. But the king was moved to pity and forgave him his debt. No sooner had this servant gone out than he came upon another who owed him a small sum and, fiercely grabbing him by the throat, he had him cast into prison. The master having heard this brought harsh justice upon him saying: "You wicked servant! I forgave you all that debt because you besought me; and should you not have had mercy on your fellow servant, as I had mercy on you?"

We must carefully note the progression of the parable. It is not because I forgive the sins of those who are in my debt that God forgives my own. I cannot exact God's forgiveness. It is because God forgives me and leads me back to Himself, because He enables me to exist, in freedom, in His grace, and because I am so overwhelmed with gratitude that I then free others from my egocentric ways and let them live in the freedom of grace as well.

We are constantly expecting something from others. They owe us their love, their attention, or their admiration. My interest is not in others but in my self-gratification, which they provide. The stuff of which I am made is vanity and irritability. And since others are a perpetual disappointment, since they cannot settle their debts with me, I pursue them out of spite and bear towards them dark and negative feelings, I get lost in a wilderness of ill-defined "vendettas." Or else, nursing my offended dignity, I remove myself, taking on an air of proud indifference and pay myself for the offenses of others...in fool's gold!

Psychologically, there is no way out of this world sealed shut by death. But if we understand that this world is an empty tomb filled with a transcendent light, and if we understand that God, in Christ, frees us from our most fundamental debt: that is death—physical death and, above all, spiritual death—then we no longer have any need of slaves to make us believe that we are gods.

We understand that others owe us nothing. They do not belong to us. Each of us is like God in whose image he is made: free and unattainable. I can appropriate him only by taking away his freedom, that is, by denying or even killing him. There are so many ways of killing someone! But just as the unattainable God reveals Himself to me through his grace, so the unattainable "other" can reveal himself to me; and this too is grace. Then I understand that "all things are grace," as Bernanos wrote in his *Journal d'un curé de campagne* (*Diary of a Country Priest*).

True, we have among ourselves relationships regulated by law. At least externally, the law extricates our murderous impulses and regulates our interactions, protecting us from arbitrary acts. But beyond that there is only forgiveness, acceptance and, at times, dazzling splendor.

"A saint," St Symeon the New Theologian would say, "is a poor man who loves his brothers." He is poor because he is continually receiving from the hands of God. He is then able to be a neighbor to all... We are hardly saints. Nevertheless, in our daily lives, we must try, without any bitterness or self-affliction, to respect the realm of others, their solitude and their relationship with mystery.

From this perspective, the better I know a person, the more they become unknown to me. I am with them from beginning to new beginning, through beginnings that have no end. When promiscuity and the wear and tear of life or the medical, pedagogical or merely envious desire to understand too much starts to dull the novelty of my experience, I need only to focus my attention. Then, there arises an element that escapes my reasonings; the distance between the "other" and myself is reestablished, a distance that is both painful and good: it is that of revelation.

At times, in silent prayer, we must learn to assume this "null being" in which we no longer belong to ourselves, we no longer exist through ourselves but we accept ourselves, and we accept the grace of knowing that others exist, outside of us yet just as inwardly as we do; where we become, as Evagrius of Pontus has said, "separated from all and united to all."

And lead us not into temptation, but deliver us from evil (...the Evil One)

"God...tempts no one," says St James (1:13). The phrase is a Semitic expression meaning: "do not allow us to enter into temptation, lest we be carried away by it."

What is the "temptation" to which we are referring? It is first of all the temptation to murder or to commit suicide—there are so many ways to kill others or to kill one's self. It is borne out of what St Maximus the Confessor refers to as "the secret fear of death." We need enemies in order to project upon them this fundamental angst. The latter must be uncovered through a lucid "remembrance of death," a recollection in the depths of which we find, instead of the void veneered with derision, the Risen One who raises us up. The transformation of our anguish into a confidence of equal measure finally allows us, at times and to a degree, to "love our enemies," according to Jesus' initially unfathomable commandment.

But most particularly, temptation is the mystery of ultimate apostasy. It is a mystery that is common to every age of Christianity because we have been in the "end times" since the Incarnation and Pentecost. As St John says: "you have heard that antichrist is coming, so now many antichrists have come" (1 Jn 2:18). Perhaps this mystery is becoming clearer in this day and age that is truly an apocalypse within history and that has revealed such atrocities. This may be simply because it is *our* age, and that it is no more "apocalyptic" than any other (the study of historical crises makes this clear).

The great apostasy is not necessarily atheism. Rebellion and even blasphemy have their own way of seeking

God. Considering the pain of this world, there is also an atheism of compassion, which is undoubtedly what is being expressed in the *Eli, Eli, lema sabachtani* spoken on Golgotha. The great apostasy is rather the sense of having "gotten over" God, of having "gotten over" the whole question, *to be removed from the mystery, devoid of any anguish or bewilderment.*

The issue is not merely the absence of God, or rather an unperturbed lack of awareness of His presence, but the perversion of the human desire for an absolute as it is captivated by horrid and seductive parodies: magic; drugs; extreme sensations; torture and eroticism (which are in fact closely connected); the lure of totalitarianism; the current development of religions into ideologies; communion, as it is so often represented in contemporary art forms and in so many sectarian circles, being replaced by assimilation and possession; the invasion of parapsychology and occultism that soon lead to mass fascination with pseudo-miracle-workers whose feats reveal power and strength such as Jesus rejected in the desert.

This calls to mind Vladimir Soloviev's *Récit sur l'Antéchrist* [The Story of Antichrist], in which the Antichrist, a great social reformer and spiritual master, takes to himself a wise man who gives "marvels and wonders" to mankind. Or Nietzsche's "last man," from the prologue of Zarathustra. "Look! I present to you the last man—Love? Creation? Desire? A star? what is it? Thus asks the last man with a wink. 'We have invented happiness,' say the last men... A little poison here and there, so as to have pleasant dreams. And finally, lots of poison, so as to die pleasantly... we have our small pleasures for day time, our small pleasures for night time; but we have respect for health—'We invented happiness, say the last men, with a wink.'"

I had the privilege of meeting and hearing Andrei Tarkovski, the director of *Andrei Rublev,* among other works. As he said, the danger in our day is *that we drop the whole question.* He expressed his commitment to awakening people and to making them understand that man *is* a question. He also said how alone he felt.

We must remain in anguish and bewilderment without pacifying ourselves with words or idols; we must continue to ask questions, even if it costs us a measure of our sanity. Why has the Church never been able to welcome people like Nietzsche, or Artaud, or Khalil Gibran, or Kazantzakis? Is it not time for the Church to offer a place to those who raise questions?

"Lead us not into temptation": the temptation to forget you, to think we have no need of you, to create subtle or grotesque parodies of you, all of which are ultimately grotesque.

"…but deliver us from evil…"

The world dwells in evil. This evil is not simply chaos or an absence of being but reflects a perverse intelligence which, through systematic, senseless horrors, intends to make us doubt God, to doubt His goodness. It is, in fact, not only the "lack of good," as the Fathers would say, nor simply a "failure to be," but the Evil One, that which is evil: neither matter nor the body, but the highest intelligence closed in upon its own light…

Adorno wrote that, after Auschwitz—I would add after Hiroshima and after the Gulag—we ought no longer to write poetry. I believe that we can, that we must continue. I believe that we can and must continue to speak of God, but perhaps in a different way. It must be noted that God did not create evil, nor did He even allow it. An expression of Léon Bloy often taken up by Berdyaev says that "the face of God is streaming with blood in the shadows."

Evil flies in the face of God, like the scourging of the blindfolded Jesus. The cries of Job can still be heard and Rachel weeps for her children. But the answer to Job has been given and remains given: *it is the Cross*. It is God crucified upon all the evil in the world but causing an immense power of resurrection to burst forth in the darkness. Pascha is the Transfiguration taking place in the abyss. "Deliver us from evil" means: Come, Lord Jesus; come, you who have come already to conquer hell and death; you who said that you "saw Satan fall like lightning from heaven" (Lk 10:18). This victory is present within the depths of the Church. We receive its strength and its joy whenever we receive communion. If Christ keeps it secret it is in order to bind us to it. "Deliver us from evil" is an active prayer intended to challenge us.

The entire Church is engaged in this ultimate battle whose aim is not victory but rather the revelation of victory. It involves all of us, from monastics who seek out hand-to-hand combat with the powers of darkness, making monasteries and hermitages to be a kind of spiritual lightning rod for the world, to the least among us who, huddled in fear against the cross of Christ, patiently attempt, day after day, to struggle against every form of evil within us, around us, in our culture and in our society, who patiently mend the fabric of life that is being continually sundered by the one to whom the Scriptures refer as "the Lord of death."

Every action that is pure goodness, neither ideological nor born of a sense of obligation, every act of justice and compassion, every spark of beauty, and every word of truth further wears away the crust under which Christ's victory over the "divider" remains hidden. We must not forget that when we speak of the Evil One, it is not to our neighbor that we must look but first to ourselves. We must not forget either that the greatest, most realistic spiritual masters—Saint Isaac of Syria, for example, or the "fool for Christ" to whom the "Siberian Missionary" refers—precisely those who had S hell, did not only pray saying "deliver us from evil" or "from the Evil One," but also "if it is possible, deliver the Evil One from evil, for he also is your creature…"

And for those of us who are ashamed of being Christians or, on the contrary, use Christianity—use our confession—as the banner of our superiority and our disdain: "deliver us from evil."

For those of us who speak of "deification" and are yet so far from being human: "deliver us from evil."

For those of us who speak so easily of love and yet are unable even to show respect for one another: "deliver us from evil."

And I who am an anguished and tormented man, so often divided, so unsure of my own existence and who yet dare to speak—with the Church; that is my only excuse—of the Kingdom and of its joy: "deliver me from evil" (Rev 21:4).

"O Only One, do not take from me the memory of this suffering on the day that you cleanse me of my evil and of my good and charge your own, the joyous ones, to clothe me with sunlight" (O. V. de L. Milosz).

St Francis de Sales predicted that at a decisive point in history there would come the *decatenatio sanctorum:* "unfettering" and the "unleashing of the saints." Today, that is both our prayer and our hope. Now the union in Christ—true God and true man—of traditional contemplations and the modern adventure, as well as the encounter between Eastern and Western Christians, are undoubtedly as favorable a set of conditions as any for this *decatenatio.* It is now Holy Saturday, when the descent into hell becomes the victory over hell; when Christ's return is being prepared, or rather the return of the cosmos and of mankind, through Christ, to the Father, so that He might finally "wipe away every tear from [our] eyes."

"For Thine is the Kingdom, and the Power, and the Glory," meaning the cross, the love and the life that is ultimately victorious; the Orthodox add "Father, Son and Holy Spirit...unto ages of ages. Amen."

II

O Heavenly King

O Heavenly King,
the Comforter,
the Spirit of Truth,
who art everywhere
and fillest all things,
treasury of blessings
and giver of life,
come and abide in us
and cleanse us from every impurity
and save our souls,
O Thou who art good
and lovest mankind.

O Heavenly King

This is the most common prayer to the Holy Spirit in the
Orthodox Church. We never begin any important activity, whether in church or in the world, without saying it.
Within the Church it is the prayer that leads into every
prayer because every authentic prayer unfolds within the
breath of the Spirit. "The Spirit helps us in our weakness;
for we do not know how to pray as we ought, but the Spirit
himself intercedes for us with sighs too deep for words"
(Rom 8:26). The point applies also to our prayer in the
world where only the Spirit can unite that which is visible
to that which is invisible; both of which, according to
Maximus the Confessor,[1] must be symbols of one another—a figure of Christ.

Christ exists within the Spirit and imparts Him to us.
His ecclesial body is the place from which this gift
springs forth, or perhaps flows out bit by bit. With His
unction Jesus anoints the members of His Body, making
them Christ-like and making of them a prophetic people.
While Pentecost is inaugurated on the occasion symboli-
cally described in the Acts of the Apostles, it is not limited to that day. It continues on, unfolding or burrowing

1 Mystagogy, 2.

deep, through what is ultimately an undauntable zeal, toward the ultimate One. It does so at times in secret and at times bursting forth, preparing and anticipating, through the Eucharist and through eucharistic beings, the return of all things to Christ.

O Heavenly King, the Comforter, the Spirit of Truth

The word "king" affirms the Spirit's divinity as the Second Ecumenical Council did in 381. The Spirit is not an anonymous force, whether created or uncreated, He is God: a unique "mode of existence" of divinity, a mysterious divine "hypostasis.

"O heavenly king…" "Heavenly," in this case, refers to the "Ocean of Divinity," as the Syriac tradition holds. The king is one who reigns. The Spirit of the Father rests in the Son. He is "the Kingdom of the Father and the Anointing of the Son," as St Gregory of Nyssa says[2]—among many others. He governs, meaning that He serves, the communion of the divine "hypostases" of whom He is "the Third," as Tradition reveals in searching the Scriptures. There is the One, the Father, and the Other, the Son, while the surpassing of any opposition is achieved in the Third. The Other is not absorbed back into the One, as seems so often to be the case in eastern spiritualities and gnostic beliefs, but there exists a thrice-holy difference within a complete coinherence.

At the same time, this King comes to us to convey all that is heavenly, to comfort us and to bestow upon us the

---

2 *De l'oraison dominicale,* 3. Cf. Paul Florensky, *La Colonne et le Fondement de la vérité,* tr. fr. Lausanne, 1975, p. 94. s.

life of resurrection. This is why in John's Gospel, during the Farewell Discourse, Christ refers to Him as Paraclete. This is often translated as Counselor, but the better expression in English is Comforter, the One who comforts by giving genuine strength. Jesus says "the other Comforter" because they are inseparable: the tremendous consolation, the sharing of lives and the flow of power inherent in Christ are poured out and manifested by the Spirit throughout history, to the measure of every sort of quest, anguish and intuition that either tear it apart or exalt it.

O Heavenly King, the Comforter: in the Spirit, God transcends His own transcendence according to a loving "trans-descendence," if I may coin an expression. Though He is altogether inaccessible, God gives Himself as a gift, becoming altogether One of whose existence we might partake. As Vladimir Lossky would say, God "crosses the boundary of His transcendence" in the Holy Spirit through whom and in whom the *Logos,* the Word, continually manifests Himself through a multitude of expressions of Wisdom and prophecy as "the light that enlightens every man coming into the world."[3] It is this same Spirit through whom and in whom the Word continues to be made flesh: for the Incarnation of the Word is effected through the Spirit—and through the lucid and powerful freedom of the Virgin, for the Spirit cannot be separated from freedom.

This is why, when we say "Spirit *of Truth,*" or rather "of the Truth," we are not referring to a notion or a set of

3 This is how one might translate verse 9 of St John's Prologue.

concepts or a system of some sort—there are so many of those!—but to *Someone* who told us that He was, that he is "the Way, the Truth and the Life." And within this One, who is the True One, the Faithful One, the Truthful One, the words "way" and "life" seem to refer especially to the Holy Spirit.

The Truth, the revelation in which the truth about God and the truth about man cannot be separated, is the Word incarnate—God made man. He is the One whose presence the Spirit imparts to us in the sacraments, the "mysteries" of the Church; within the Church which is itself the mystery of the Risen One, the sacrament of the resurrection through the grace of the Holy Spirit.

Christ journeys with those on their way to Emmaus, but they do not recognize Him. And yet his words, borne upon His breath, makes their hearts burn within them. At the breaking of the eucharistic bread, He reveals Himself and at once is gone from their sight. Henceforth, He can be present only in the Holy Spirit. This is why the Church, the Body of Christ, is also the Temple of the holy Spirit. In Christ, the Church is *the Church of the Holy Spirit*.

Who art everywhere and fillest all things

Grace penetrates all things as they tremble and resonate and awaken in this tremendous Breath of life, like a tree in the wind, with sweeping, invisible strokes, like the ocean with its thousands of smiling ripples, or the impulse that moves man and woman toward one another. Modern idiom tends to oppose spirit and matter, while a kind of pseudo-platonism opposes the intelligible and the tangible. But the Holy Spirit—*Ruach* in Hebrew, *Pneuma* in Greek and *Spiritus* in Latin—is the Breath, the Wind that blows where it wills and whose sound we hear (Jn 3:8) for it bears the Word and within it the world itself, both visible and invisible.

In semitic languages, the word *Ruach* is sometimes masculine and sometimes feminine. We would not want to reduce the Trinity, or "naturalize" it into some sort of familial construct: Father, Mother and Son, but we must recognize the confused expressions of our language: the virile nature of the fire of the Spirit, and the feminine character of the "still small voice"[4] like a mother humming her child to sleep.

Perhaps here we gain a sense for the mysterious wisdom present throughout the last books of the Old Testament, reminding us that God is *rahamim*, the emphatic plural form of *rehem*, which means "womb."

St Maximus the Confessor evokes the presence of the Holy Spirit in the very existence of the world, in beings and in things that are all *logoi* of the *Logos*, words addressed to us by God. In his Epistle to the Ephesians (4:6), Paul speaks of God as being above all and through all and in all. It is true that the Father is always the transcendent God, the principle of all reality. The Word is the *Logos* who orders the world through His creative ideas/will. And the Spirit is truly God in all things, enlivening and leading all things to their ultimate fulfillment in beauty. He is the winged God, so represented through symbols of movement and flight: the wind, a bird, the

4 1 Kg 19:12.

living water; yet not earth but rather He who makes the earth into a sacrament.

Treasury of blessings and giver of life

The word "blessings," just like the word "good" at the end of this prayer, has an ontological meaning that has to do with being, or love as it were, for "God is love," as St John says. Thus being is nothing other than the depth and inexhaustible substance of this love. One might say that being is relational and akin to the inwardness (and the radiance) of communion. Thus, the blessings which the Spirit imparts, those of which He is the "treasury,"—meaning the locus of giving and of dissemination— are grace, the life of resurrection and "the light of life," again as St John says. "The Holy Spirit becomes within us all that the Scriptures say concerning the Kingdom of God: a pearl, a grain of mustard seed, leaven, water, fire, the bread and the draught of life, the wedding chamber..."[5]

This is why the text of this prayer qualifies the word "blessings"—which might be thought of as something static—with the word "life." The Spirit, as the Nicaean-Constantinopolitan Creed says, is the "giver of life." Whenever we speak of the Spirit, "life" seems to be the key word. In Greek, there are two distinct terms: *bios,* in reference to biological life, and *zoe,* in reference to spiritual life, or perhaps, more along the lines of foundation and fulfillment, through the resurrected life in Christ. And yet, it is perhaps best if we do not distinguish too sharply between the two, but regard them as ever-in-

5   St Symeon the New Theologian, *Sermon 90.*

creasing degrees and intensity. Every living thing is
moved by the divine Breath. And so it is with this invisible framework that is in constant motion and causes the
universal tendency toward dissolution, chaos and en-
tropy to be turned back into a reintegration, a more and
more refined complexity, in such a way that life is continually born out of death. This is a fundamental figure
of the Cross, of death and resurrection. A great physician
once said that the world is flowing with intelligence! The
Spirit is present and active in every living thing, from the
cell-stage to mystical union, through the great movement
of *eros* which touches and intensifies every existence
and, through man, leads all toward grace, toward *agape*.

And yet, while we can say that all life within the
world is sustained by the Spirit, by His energy which has
long remained, and often still is, anonymous, this life is
still linked to death. But ever since Christ's resurrection,
the personal source of this *Spirit* is henceforth revealed.
Or rather hidden-revealed, which may serve as a defini-
tion of the sacrament, or it would already be the Parousia.
Nevertheless, in the eucharistic chalice the Spirit imparts
a pure life, one which assumes death and, one might say,
turns it back. Thus, every partial death—the inevitable
stigma of our existence—and ultimately our biological
death, are henceforth *paschas*, or passages of initiation: it
is the veil of love, slowly torn asunder. Death, in its full-
est meaning, that is both physical and spiritual, is in a
sense already passed, shrouded in the waters of our baptism (or perhaps also in desire, in tears, and in blood).
The ultimate stage of our existence is no longer death but
the Spirit. And if we pay close attention to this presence,

if we seek it out down to its greatest depths of silence, of peace and of light, then the anguish within us is turned to trust and our tears become a wedding garment, the robe of the beggar who, purely by grace, is invited to the feast.

The Spirit is also the hidden God, the secret and interior God, a transcendence identified with the very root of our being. He is the welling up within our hearts which becomes a testimony enabling us to say that Christ is the Lord and to whisper with Him and in Him, *Abba* Father—a word full of tenderness, trust and respect. The Spirit kindles our hearts, revealing within us the "eye of the heart," the "eye of fire" which discloses in each of us the image of God and, in all things, the "burning bush" of the coming Christ. "The eye through which I see God and the eye through which God sees me are one and the same eye," as Meister Eckhart would say.[6] And this one eye is the Spirit in Christ who is truly God and truly man. The prison of time and space is weakening; we find ourselves breathing more deeply, with an overwhelming joy, we are "breathing the Spirit," in the admirable words of St Gregory of Sinai.[7] Thus, becoming progressively "separated from all and united to all,"[8] we truly begin to love with a love that is neither about loss nor about acquisition.

The eye of the heart, when it is opened by the Spirit, discerns Christ as the latent root of every religion as well as of every form of humanism and atheism, providentially rebelling against any number of caricatures of God.

---

6 *Sermon 12.*
7 *Petite philocalie de la prière du coeur,* 1re ed., Paris, 1953, p. 250.
8 Evagrius Ponticus, in I. Hausherr, *Les Leçons d'un Contemplatif,* 1960, p. 187.

The eye of the heart sees not only the Church within the world—so often a pitiful sociological construct—but the world within the Church; a Church without boundaries where the communion of saints extends to a communion with every great living being, creators of life, of justice and of beauty.

At the heart of this boundless Church, of this "boundless love," as the "Monk of the Eastern Church" entitled his most beautiful work," we perceive and celebrate Mary, the Mother of God; the one who, by receiving the Spirit in order to give birth to the Word, undid the tragedy of human freedom. For once our freedom welcomes the Spirit, He makes it free and fertile, giving it an infinite space for creation and molding it within eternity. This is why the Orthodox Church uses the same expression to describe both the Spirit and the Virgin: the Spirit is *panhagion*, all-holy, and the Virgin is *panhagia*.

Come and abide in us

After affirming that the Spirit is everywhere and filling all things, our prayer then moves us to implore Him: *Come*. If we must, in this way, call upon the One who calls us, it stands to reason that He who fills all things does not fill us.

When God creates and sustains the world, He removes Himself in a way, so as to give His creatures their own foundation. This *separation*, according to the Fathers, is an integral part of human freedom—as well as of that of angels who augment mankind's rejection and the willing exile of the "prodigal son" to cosmic proportions. Thus, the beauty of the world, which was once a celebration, becomes magical, nostalgic and burdened with sadness, ever-further slipping into a hopeless torpor. And so also, the magnificence of *eros* may turn to a possessive rage, a drug, leading us to destroy without ever truly knowing the other. The Spirit, though He bears us up and gives us life, surrounding us like an atmosphere that is ready to penetrate the slightest fissure within our souls, cannot do so without our consent, our call. We must pray: Come.

"Come, O unknowable One; Come, O unceasing joy, Come, O unwaning light... Come, O resurrection of the dead... Come, O you who remain ever the same and who, at every hour, moves and draws near to us who lay in hades... Come, O my breath and my life."[9] Such is indeed the human condition; our prayer becomes more specific.

The world abides in the Spirit. This universe that we can probe to depths of billions of light years, St Benedict of Nursia suddenly glimpsed as a speck of dust within a ray of divine light. St Gregory the Great recounted this vision in *Dialogues*, while St Gregory Palamas understood this ray of light as the divine energies shining forth through the Holy Spirit. Creation exists only by the will, the love and the protection of God who, at the same time, is excluded by mankind from the heart of this creation—because that heart is man himself. We may then suggest that if creation has its abode within God, He cannot have his abode within creation, for man has retained, as it were, a perverted, luciferian guardianship of the keys: he is able to close the universe off to God. And thus the forces of evil arise, paradoxically given substance.

9   St Symeon the New Theologian, Preface to *Hymns of Divine Love*.

Mary gave a "city," a dwelling place, back to God, the "king without a city."[10] She enabled him to be incarnate within the heart of His own creation, as if to recreate it. As Nicholas Cabasilas would say: "God created the world to find a mother." Mankind welcomes its God through freedom, within Mary's womb. Jesus has no stone upon which to lay His head, lest it be in the "marian" love of those who welcome Him. The Spirit, from all eternity the abode of the Son, can make of each one of us the abode of the incarnate Son, on one fundamental condition—that we pray: "*come and abide in us, and cleanse us from every impurity.*"

And cleanse us from every impurity

Perhaps all we need is a spark of joy mixed with gratitude or, before the "walls" of Hippolytus[11] or Sartre, an anguished sigh to dissolve our conceit, or perhaps to recoil in the face of horror—No! I will not take part in this—or a child's gaze whose bewildered innocence pierces our defenses, or even a moment of peace during which our heart awakens; there are only faces: the hidden face of the world, a heavenly earth, the world as sacrament to which I referred earlier in the context of the ecstasy of one such as Alyosha Karamazov, that is both heavenly and earthly.

If any of the Beatitudes is favored among the spiritual minds of the Christian East, it would be "Blessed are the pure in heart for they shall see God." This Beatitude is not of a moral character, as it is all too often interpreted, but of

---

10 St Nicholas Cabasilas, in his *Marian Homilies*.
11 In Dostoievsky's *The Idiot*.

openness and clarity of the "eye of the heart": it is a tarnished mirror in need of cleaning and polishing, a wellspring buried beneath the rubble of a fallen life that must be removed in order to allow the living water to flow forth.

The heart is the innermost center where man's entire being—his mind, his fervor and his desire—is called to gather itself up and surpass itself within God. It must be cleansed not only of "evil thoughts," of reprehensible obsession, but of all thought. And thus immersed in its own light, which can be no more than a transparent medium, the awareness of one's conscience becomes a void, purely receptive, a cup that is offered up, a humble chalice into which the flame of the Spirit descends to recreate us—an interiorized Pentecost.

This theme of impurity—of corruption, as the ascetics would say—brings us back to the most fundamental texts of the Gospel, to the evangelical revolution that sets mankind free from the infinitely complex and codified scheme of the sacred and the profane, the pure and the impure. What makes a man impure, as Jesus says, is not the omission of the ritual washing of hands, nor is it that which one consumes according to a prescription of acceptable and forbidden foods. St Augustine was a Manichean for several years; he had been taught a gnosis by which to distinguish between darkness and light—the darkness of ham, for example and the light of a melon! And in this day and age, the more we stuff ourselves, the more we seek similar distinctions, as the sacred amounts to a slender body we wish always to keep young!

Nevertheless, as Jesus says, what renders a man impure is what comes out of his mouth, proceeding from the heart: *dialogismoi*, the blind play of fear, of hatred, of a narcissistic libido, of greed and of "folly." These suggestions rise up from the heart, from the depths of the subconscious mind; from our own, but also on a collective level, according to the latest political trends. We must learn to cast them into the fire of the Spirit, that they be either consumed or transfigured... This is how we can kill impurity and corruption at their roots, which are none other than death in its plethora of disguises. Impurity then seems to be all that causes isolation and confusion, that impedes and diverts the powers of life, that keeps man from understanding that he is in need of being saved lest he die and find nothing but the void or the nightmares within it. It is all that keeps us from understanding that we make up a single Adam, as members of the same Body and members of one another. It is because we are incapable of cleansing ourselves of this filth that we must call on the Spirit: *Come and cleanse us from every impurity.*

Although this is quite a significant effect, the highest level of psychoanalysis can do no more than open our eyes to the dynamics and the emphasis we place on our desires and on death; it affects the potential adjustments which alleviate our suffering, the way we might move the weight of a burden from one shoulder to the other. But there is no genuine freedom from it. Freud regarded Hermholtz as his god for having discovered the law of the conservation of energy. This vital, psychic energy, which remains in flux but is never diminished, can be at peace and be transformed into paschal joy only through the coming of grace, the coming of the Spirit. The seal of death is shattered. This time, we will not settle for rearranging the furniture, we will open the windows and let in the Wind from afar come in and purify the atmosphere.

Yes! We must entreat the Spirit *de profundis,* from the depths of the earth, through a whole-hearted ascesis—one of trust and humility.

And save our souls

To save someone—meaning to make them safe, to make them whole (or holy)—thus consists in freeing them from death and hell, from this "dead life" which we so often confuse with life itself, from murdering others and one's self and, undoubtedly, from murdering God. Man is created from nothingness; if he allows himself to be overwhelmed by fear or by a desperate, climactic flight from this fear, he proceeds toward illusion, toward his dreams, or to an unresolvable insight into an offended love.

Christ descends into hell and into death, into the nocturnal abyss where being is overcome, in order to tear from its grasp each of us and all of mankind. By making our wounds His own, Christ turns every wound within us into a source of light—the "light of life," the light of the Holy Spirit. In Cana, Christ transforms our life-blood into wine suffused with the Holy Spirit. He gives the land of the living to those who do not bury their "talents" but multiply them. Salvation is not only a deliverance but a quickening.

Thus, when the prayer says: *Save our souls*, it is not referring to spiritualism, to a salvation consisting in freeing the soul from its bodily prison. The soul, in this case, refers to the person that transcends and gives existence to our entire being, making it either opaque or luminous.

Even slavery can be transformed from horror into blasphemy or into a cry of faith, as seen in the contrast between the thieves crucified, one on the right and one on the left of Christ. Again we could say that the soul is life unified, where the visible becomes the symbol of the invisible, and the invisible the meaning of the visible. It can be clearly seen in certain scriptural passages where we know whether to translate using "soul" or "life." The soul that is saved—mingled with the breath of the Spirit—beginning with the heart ("the body in the depths of one's body," as Palamas would say[12]), suffuses all of our faculties, all of our senses and even the human and cosmic environment.

"Though my body is dying, never have I felt so alive..." Thus is prepared and anticipated through abundance of life the resurrection of the dead, in the unity of the whole Adam, and the transfiguration of the cosmos: the Holy Spirit, the Spirit of resurrection—the unknown One—will fully reveal Himself through the communion of faces, of bodies become faces, souls will draw from the earth, the "image of the image," bodies that are both faithful to what they once were and renewed in the Ultimate One.

Save our souls, O Thou

The culmination of the prayer is this "Thou," which reminds us that the Spirit is a "person," hidden but nevertheless real, whom we hear speaking and whom we see

---

12 Cf. J. Meyendorff, *Introduction à l'étude de Grégoire Palamas*, Paris, 1959, p. 211.

acting in the Acts of the Apostles. We must emphasize that we are not speaking of a person in the psychological and social sense that the term has acquired, but of a "hypostasis," meaning God Himself becoming out breath, our unfathomable depth and our life. Between our stifling inherence within the world of objects and our indomitable certainty that we are *something other* lies this indestructible flame—the Spirit.

Thus the conclusion:

O Thou who art good and lovest mankind

We must go back to the ontological connotations of the word "good," both in Hebrew and in Greek. In Genesis, at the end of each day that represents a part of the process of creation, we read: "And God saw that is was *tob*." This word means both beautiful and good. This is why in the Greek version of the Septuagint, dated between the fifth and the second century BC, *tob* is translated as *kalon*, which means beautiful, and not as *agathon*, which means good. It refers to the fullness of being that is created and recreated by the Word, animated and fulfilled by the Spirit, thus reflecting divine life. Through man who, in Christ, has become once again the created creator, that fullness of being is called to unite itself to this divine life. It is the word of an artisan, or a peasant for whom good, if it is truly good, is necessarily beautiful. Let us abandon our aesthetic distinctions: old tools were beautiful because they were useful.

The goodness-beauty of the Spirit refers to the delight of God in His creation, a delight which causes both the unity and the diversity of His creation. According to

Dionysius the Areopagite, the activity of the Spirit consists precisely in this trinitarian outpouring in the world
of Uni-Diversity, such that the multiplicity is set at odds
that it might be brought back together, not in the form of
an undifferentiated synthesis, but into a harmony that is
all the more vibrant for having originated in the extreme
tension of opposites. Truly, in the Spirit "things opposed
to one another are reconciled, says Heraclitus, from
things which differ from one another arises the most
beautiful harmony..."[13] For it is not only unity, as in
muddled spiritualities, but also the diversity which
comes from God and identifies Him. In the unity of
Christ the Spirit of goodness and beauty eternally pre-
serves the unique form of every creature: "Their whole
being shall be saved and live in all its fullness forever."[14]
The Spirit, Serge Bulgakov used to say, is the Hypostasis
of Beauty, a beauty that expresses *the power of goodness*.

At this point the theme of *deification* comes into play:
"God became man that man might become God," as the
Fathers would say, not by casting off his humanity but by
giving it its fullness in Christ, through the fire of the Spirit.
Athanasius of Alexandria would put it still more accu-
rately: "God became *sarkophoros* (flesh-bearer) that man
might become *pneumatophoros* (Spirit-bearer)."[15] The
soul of one who has been sanctified, suffused with the
Breath of God—to use approximate, though significant,
spatial terminology—is no longer within the body, it is
rather the body that is within the soul and, through it, in

---

13 *Fragment 8.*
14 St Dionysios the Areopagite, *On the Divine Names*, VIII, 9.
15 *On the Incarnation and Against the Arians. PG* 26, 996.

the Spirit. The primal clay has become a "spiritual body," both body and Breath.

The goodness of the Spirit does not manifest itself only through the transfiguration—at times quite apparent—of the saints, but also through each humble gesture that enduringly refashions every being whom hatred and cruelty have torn apart. The Spirit is the great mender of daily life.

The beauty of the Spirit is expressed in the quality of a gaze devoid of judgment that is welcoming and that sustains life.

O Thou who art goodness, O Thou who art beauty, O Thou who art fullness in the sacrament of this moment, come! O Thou who art the breath of my breath and the "life of my life," as St Augustine would say.

At the heart of every sacramental action, particularly the Eucharist, there must be an *epiclesis*, the supplication addressed to the Father, the source of the Divinity, that He send forth His Holy Spirit "upon us and upon these gifts here offered"—the bread and the wine in the case of the Eucharist—that the assembly of people, as it makes an offering and is itself offered up, might be integrated into the body of Christ.

The prayer which I have just discussed rather awkwardly is an immeasurable epiclesis; an epiclesis upon all of humanity and the cosmos, for the advent of the Kingdom which, according to an ancient form of the Our Father is none other than the Holy Spirit.

III

The Prayer of Saint Ephrem

O Lord and Master of my life,
take from me the spirit of sloth,
despair, lust of power and idle talk;
grant rather the spirit of chastity, humility,
patience and love to thy servant.
Yea, O Lord and King,
grant me to see my own transgressions
and not to judge my brother,
for blessed art Thou unto ages of ages.
Amen.

The Prayer of Saint Ephrem

This prayer is attributed to St Ephrem the Syrian (306-ca. 373) and is a significant element of the services of Great Lent. It is repeated three times, accompanied by three great "metania," the prostrations in which the forehead touches the floor. Metania (*metanoia*) refers specifically to penitence as a conversion of our entire perception of reality.

O Lord and Master of my life

"Lord" suggests the inaccessible mystery of "God beyond God," the *hypertheos*. And yet this God is no stranger to me; I exist by His will; His Breath enlivens the earth from which I was made; He calls me and elicits a response; through His incarnation He has become "master of my life." It is He who gives my life meaning even—and especially—when the meaning eludes me. In this context the term "Master," while emphasizing transcendence, does not refer to a tyrant but to a sacrificing and liberating Father whose desire is to adopt me in His Son, and who bears an unlimited respect for my freedom. The incarnate Son, in whom the Father is fully present, is born in a stable, allows Himself to be murdered by our cruel freedom, then rises again revealing Himself only to those who love Him.

Nevertheless, this crucified "master" remains the master of all life. He alone can free us from our freedom; He alone can transfigure the dark passions of our lives into His life-giving Breath. The greatness of this king lies in the fact that He makes Himself our servant: "I am among you as one who serves."

Thus my relationship with the Master is not one of servitude but one of free trust. He is the "Master of my life" because He is its source, because I am continually receiving it from Him, and because it is He who gives and forgives, and continues to give in abundance a future made new: "Go, and sin no more." I exist only through this ultimately subtle love which bears me up unconditionally and beyond any need; a love that makes itself a servant, that those who wish to serve it might become its friends. The ascetic effort that is stressed during Great Lent can only be a genuine liberation within the context of faith…and faith entails first and foremost risking a measure of trust. In you, O Master of my life, who reveal yourself as a countenance, I place all my trust; in your word and in your presence, for you are not merely an example but the undivided One who becomes our place of rest, a place devoid of death: "Come to me all you who labor and are heavy-laden and I will give you rest." You are a place for us who are orphans of our native earth and of wise customs, You are the place wherein is life, You are its Master. In this place we will dig out the catacombs from which the cathedrals of the future will rise up.

Take from me the spirit of sloth, despair, lust of power and idle talk

There is a way. You are the way. But along this way are obstacles which define our fundamentally sinful condition; a condition of which Jesus reminded those who wished to stone the woman caught in adultery.

"Sloth," in this instance, is not of the kind we experience on a lazy summer vacation. Sloth means forgetfulness, to which the ascetics refer as "the greatest of all sins." Forgetfulness means the inability to be amazed, to marvel or even to see. It is a kind of slumber, a form of sleepwalking, whether expressed in hyperactivity or in inertia. It is a frame of mind in which the only relevant criteria become utility, profitability and the correlation of price and quality. There are interior as well as exterior hindrances: an over-crowded agenda for some, where every activity leads to another, and insufficient involvement for others who fall prey to violence and drugs. I may forget that others have as deep an inward existence as I do; I may never stop for anything; I may never be captivated by music or by a rose; I may never give thanks—since all things are rightfully mine. I may forget that all things are rooted in mystery and that mystery dwells within me. I may forget God and His creation. I may no longer know how to accept myself as a creature with an immeasurable destiny. I may forget death and the possible meaning beyond it. All this amounts to a spiritual neurosis which has to do not with sexuality—which may become the means of forgetting—but with suppressing the "light of life" which gives meaning to others, to the smallest spec of dust as well as to myself.

This forgetfulness, having developed into a collective phenomenon, can only yield dreadful consequences. We convince ourselves that God does not exist, and the neurosis becomes more intense. Out of the void, the fallen angels begin to pervade history. O Lord and Master of my life, awaken me!

This "sloth," this anesthetic which affects our whole being, this insensitivity, the closing off of the depths of our heart, the sexual and intellectual frustration, all these lead to "despondency." It is what the ascetics refer to as "accedia"—an aversion to life; despair. What is the use of anything? Nowadays there is a fascination with suicide, and derision is universal. I have "gotten over" everything; it is all the same to me; I have become cynical and numb. I am very old and no longer have the spirit of childhood.

We may as well turn and run, flee toward the spirit of "lust of power" and that of "idle talk." We need slaves and enemies. We invent them. We lord over others to feel as if we were gods, we have enemies in order to hold them responsible for our anxiety. Torturing others—as it is always their fault—violating their bodies and perhaps even their souls, keeping them at our mercy, on the verge of extinction but without letting them escape into death—this is the experience of a nearly-divine omnipotence. In them, I hate my own mortality. As I trample them down, I trample down my own death. There have been god-kings and deified tyrants—every display of power takes on a sacred character.

This is why, at the cost of their lives, the first Christians refused to call Caesar lord. Only God is Lord. Other

Christians from this century have refused to worship race or class and have paid the price. Christ stripped power of its sacred character by reminding us to render to God what is God's, and to Caesar what is Caesar's. Over the centuries Christians have not always lived up to this. They once blessed an emperor who had killed his son and his wife because they believed he had placed his power in God's service. In some instances, the hope that power might become a means of service is gratified; most often, it is a costly illusion.

And to what degree has the lust for power contaminated even the Church? "Idle talk"—an expression taken from the Gospels—refers to every thought, to every bit of imagination that withdraws from silence, from wonder, from the intensity of *being*, and from mystery. It refers to any approach to man that claims to explain and simplify him without taking into account all that is in him that cannot be explained or simplified; any approach to creation which does not account for its rhythm and beauty. It is understanding rather than inspiration; the illusions of an art that is attempting to divest itself of its nuptial quality.

We live in a civilization of "idle talk," of idle images, where our excessive needs scuttle our desires, where money determines our dreams, where advertising has developed into the opposite of ascesis, the intentional reduction of needs for the sake of sharing and freeing one's desire. Nevertheless, we await a word of life; with the burden of silence and the awareness of death, we await a word of resurrection.

Grant rather the spirit of chastity, humility, patience and love to Thy servant

With every petition we acknowledge our condition as "servants," creatures that are recreated by a Breath that rises up from our innermost being. Prayer is not merely meditation, it is an encounter, a relationship, a "conversation," according to the old monks. God speaks to us through Scripture, through beings and things, through our life-experiences, and through His presence in such gentle words of silence, like tongues of fire in one's heart (instead of imaginary, impudent and illusory babble). Only an equal measure of prayer can break through the magical circle of *philautia*, of metaphysical narcissism, of the spirit of "lust of power" and conceit. The "virtues" listed in this prayer coexist in order to become one and are thus rooted in faith. From this perspective, "virtue" is not merely morality but a participation in Christ's humanity, a deified humanity in which the human virtues are fully realized through their union with the divine Names which they reflect.

The meaning of "chastity" is not restricted to continency, as per a moralizing and limited perspective. It refers rather to integration and integrity. A chaste man is no longer fragmented, swept up like a reed by the waves of an impersonal *eros*. He integrates *eros* into communion and the power of life into the relationships of a personal existence. For a monk, chastity does indeed mean continency (though not all continency is chaste). His *eros* is consumed in *agape*, in his encounter with the living and personal God, in his inexhaustible admiration—first in pain then in wonder—for the crucified One, the vanquisher of death.

Chastity, for a man and a woman who share a noble and faithful love, the way Christ is united to His Church and as God is betrothed to mankind and to the world, exists in the light of a trinitarian uni-diversity, the transformation of *eros*—also through *agape*—into an encounter, an expression of persons engaged in the tenderness of a patient and reciprocal discovery. And then come children, these little unknown or unexpected guests, just in time to keep this passion from closing in upon itself in a parody of the absolute.

A thought, a word or an expression is chaste insofar as they are permeated, in all honesty and realism, by this fundamental purity, respect for the body, the gathering up of life into a mystery that gives it both peace and unity. The Bible decries the impersonal ecstasy of ritual prostitution and insists upon the "Song of Songs" as an encounter that is sought, lost, then found again—for God is the One who is ever sought after, as St Gregory of Nyssa would say—and upon a humble faithfulness, for God is the ever-faithful One.

"Humility" inscribes faith into our everyday life. I have nothing that has not been given to me. The thread of my existence, that is so precarious, so often on the verge of breaking, is held together only by the strange will of some Other. Humility "is a gift of God and from God Himself," says John Climacus, "for it is said: learn neither from angels nor from men but from me—as I dwell within you, as I illumine and work within you—that I am gentle and humble of heart, in thought and in spirit, and your souls will find rest from their struggles and comfort from your thought."[1] The Publican from the parable is a

1 *The Ladder of Divine Ascent*, 25-3.

humble man. He, being scorned as a "collaborator," does not claim to be virtuous but depends solely on the mercy of God, while the Pharisee, who is all too perfect, has no need of a Savior. For a perfect, self-assured man who is proud of his uprightness, there is no room for God in the World: he himself fills all things. A humble man, however, makes room. He opens himself up to the benevolent gift of salvation, he welcomes it gratefully and wraps his heart in a festive garment.

Humility-*humus*: not oppression, but fertility. Humility is active, it tills the soil in order to yield a hundred-fold once the Sower passes by.

Humility is a virtue we may perceive in others but which we cannot see in ourselves. Anyone who says: "I am humble" is woefully vain. One becomes humble without seeking to be so, through obedience, detachment, and respect for the unconditional gift of this mystery; in a word, through openness to grace. It is achieved especially through "the fear of God," which is not like the fear of a slave dreading the chastisement of his master but rather like the sudden terror of knowing one might lose one's life in illusion, in narcissistic self-sufficiency, and in the void of the "passions." The "fear of God" makes us humble and frees us from our fear of the world—I am free because I no longer possess anything, says one character from Solzhenitsyn's *First Circle*—it is slowly transformed into the kind of wondrous fear that comes from any powerful love. Humility is expressed in one's ability to be attentive: to others, to the grain of wood, to a scorpion settled on a step or to a passing cloud...such a beautiful moment. Humility gives us the ability to be awake, "to see the secrets of the glory of God hidden in every being…"[2]

Humility is the foundation and the product of "virtue," both of which remain invisible. It is the sensitivity of one's whole being to the resurrection.

While we may be unable to know anything concerning this elusive humility, we can learn much from "patience" in humiliation. As a monk might say to those who remain in the world, that which we seek through abstinence, you will find through patience in the face of the inevitable changes and even tragedies of this existence. Patience is indeed a form of interiorized monasticism. It is the opposite of despondency, which so often stems from our adolescent desires for instant gratification. It is patience that led St Thérèse of Lisieux to transfigure her impatience into an insatiable desire for holiness. Patience puts its trust in time. Not merely ordinary time, where death has the last word and where time erodes, separates and destroys everything, but time mingled with eternity, as it is offered to us by the Resurrection. The time that moves toward death is one of anguish; the time that moves toward the Resurrection is one of hope. Thus patience remains attentive to the life-cycles which are at times paradoxical, like the grain that dies in order to bear much fruit. It knows that even experiences of death can be a new stage, a quasi-initiation breaking away from the previous one, as long as it leads us to the foot of the life-giving cross and renews in us the flow of the living waters of baptism. When it seems as though God has withdrawn, when a person's gaze strikes fear into me, or when that

2 St Isaac the Syrian, *Ascetical Homilies*, 72.

gaze turns to stone at the moment of death, when our personal as well as our collective hopes begin to crumble, then patience is our haven. In that regard it is like the love which St Paul says "bears all things, believes all things, hopes all things, endures all things." (1 Cor 13:7).

The Fathers often refer to the "patience of Job," while Dostoievsky and Berdiaev have also referred to his rebellion. This rebellion is not aimless, however, but carried out in a kind of faith. Job rejects the pleasant theodicies of armchair theologians; he knows that Someone is seeking him out through the very experience of evil. "Patience within azure," or patience in darkness, as the poet rightly says:

> "Every atom of silence
> Is a chance
> for a ripened fruit."[3]

Everything truly culminates in a "love" that is a synthesis of every "virtue," whose essence is Christ. Freeing oneself from impatient and hopeless "passions" through patience and hope enables one little by little to acquire *apatheia,* which is not stoic impassibility but an inner freedom and participation in the "foolish love" which God bears toward His creatures. According to St Symeon the New Theologian, a man who sanctifies himself becomes "a poor man filled with brotherly love."[4] He is poor because he strips himself of his roles, of his social (or ecclesiastical) importance and of his neurotic characteristics, because he opens himself up to God

---

3 Paul Valéry
4 Basil Krivocheine, *In the Light of Christ, Saint Symeon the New Theologian,* ch. 1.

and to others, without separating prayer from service. He
is then able to discern a person within others, beneath all
the masks and ugliness and sin, the way Jesus did in the
Gospels. He is able to bring peace to those who hate
themselves and who destroy the world.

The scene of the Last Judgment, in chapter 25 of St
Matthew's Gospel shows that in putting love into active
practice—feeding, welcoming, clothing, taking in, heal-
ing and freeing—there is no need to wave the divine banner, because for every man, man himself is a sacrament
of Christ, the *homo maximus*.[5] He is a secret and concrete
sacrament.

Abba Antony once said: "Life and death depend upon
our neighbor. Indeed, if we gain our brother, we gain
God. But if we scandalize our brother, we sin against
Christ."[6]

And in the words of Isaac the Syrian: "Brother, this is
what I recommend: to let the weight of compassion
within you tip the scale to the point that you might feel
within you heart God's own compassion for the world."[7]

**Yea, O Lord and King, grant me to see my own
transgressions and not to judge my brother, for
blessed art Thou unto ages of ages. Amen.**

The final request discloses and denounces one of the
forms of sin that is most terrifying, on a personal as well
as on a collective level: justifying oneself while con-
demning others, deifying oneself while damning others,

5 Nicholas of Cusa, *Sermons*, 149; *De cribatione Alchorani*, 507.
6 *Apophthegmata*, Antony, 9.
7 *Ascetical Homilies*, 34.

hating, despising and discounting others, and doing it all with a clear conscience because we are right. "To see one's own sin" is to obey the first command of the Gospel: "Repent, for the Kingdom of God is at hand." When the light does draw near, it casts out the darkness within us. One who discovers himself in this way, and whose mind and heart are converted—as these words are understood in the Bible—is able to see the extent of his deviance, of the perdition into which he leads others, of the void that awaits him and already pervades him, of the abyss over which he has laid a path that has now crumbled. Such is the "remembrance of death" to which the ascetics refer: laying bare this fundamental anguish that we repress but that is nevertheless expressed in the hatred of one's brother and in the frantic need to judge him—that is, to condemn him. But if the "remembrance of death" is suffused not with derision but with faith, this same faith, within still greater depths, discovers Christ the vanquisher of hell coming between us and the void. In Him, every separation is overcome: God's inaccessible character, sin and death. I am no longer judged but saved; I no longer need to judge but to affect salvation.

"To see one's own sin" does not consist in tallying up one's transgressions, it means feeling asphyxiated and lost, drowning, in vain thrashing about in this lost state and betraying love, scorning and laughing all the while, so great is our self-hatred. It means suffocating in the waters of death, that they might instead become baptismal waters. It is to die, but henceforth to die in Christ in order to be reborn in His breath and to regain a foothold in the Father's house. As an old saying goes, "seeing one's own

sin is a greater miracle than raising the dead." Because seeing one's own sin is like passing through the most difficult of deaths. Whereas after our baptismal rebirth, without even being aware of it, we add life unto life, having become one of those who bring peace to this existence. And yet, as staretz Silouan of Mount Athos used to say, "our hearts must shed blood" in order to challenge certain negative conceptions, to break the stone within some hearts and be able to implore God for universal salvation.

One who sees his own sin and does not judge his brother becomes capable of truly loving him. I have been disappointed in myself often enough that I can no longer be disappointed by anyone. I know that man, made in the image of God, is both Secret and Love, but that this love can turn to hate. I respect the Secret, I await nothing in return. If love should come of it, it is pure grace.

And so we must bless all things. We must attempt to become beneficent rather than possessive beings—who possess and are possessed. There is an infinite reciprocity of blessings: we bless God who blesses us; we bless all things in His light, keeping in mind that a blessing, so as not to become "idle talk," must be "beneficent." Yes! We must act upon the blessings received within our very depths, submitting ourselves to every life that life itself might grow and become a blessing.

The prayer of St Ephrem intimates the nature of ascesis: fasting, but not merely from bodily nourishment. This fasting must also be from whatever weighs upon the soul, so that we might live not by bread alone (by images, noise and excitement) but by every word that proceeds

from the mouth of God.[8] We must fast from the "passions" and from our desire to dominate and to condemn. We must do so in order to achieve the true freedom which St John Climacus was able to describe: "Be ruler of your own heart, reign in the heights of humility, commanding laughter: come, and it comes; and gentle tears: come, and they come; and the body, no longer a tyrant but a servant: do this, and it does it."[9]

---

8   Mt 4:4.
9   *The Ladder of Divine Ascent*, 7, 3.